DADDY SAID ...

DADDY SAID . . .

ANN DAVIS

Library of Congress Control Number: 2010909884
ISBN: Hardcover   978-1-4535-3291-1
                 Softcover   978-1-4535-3290-4
                 Ebook   978-1-4535-3292-8

To order additional copies of this book, contact:
Xlibris Corporation
1-888-795-4274
www.Xlibris.com
Orders@Xlibris.com
78983

Contents

Dedication

This book is dedicated to all the men and women who grew up in the fifties and sixties when the old African adage "It takes a village to raise a child" still applied. This was the way it was in my neighborhood. My neighborhood was a mixed one. Disciplining the children in my neighborhood was every adult's job and they would inform our parents. This was an unwritten rule in the community. Boy, we knew that we were in trouble. Not one parent fell out or stopped speaking because a neighbor corrected or reprimanded another's child.

This book is dedicated to my new friend Lolita Westerfield who encouraged me daily until her death to stop talking about writing *Daddy Said*. She would say, "Get your ideas on paper." "Girl, get started! I am going to remind you every week until you start your book". One day, in January 2003, she walked into my classroom, handed me a sheet of paper with the words "Dedication Page." Turned around and walked out without a word. Thanks, Lolita, I am finally getting this book done. Another colleague, Joy Clemons, and I were always comparing what our fathers said as we grew up. Joy is *much* younger than I. Nevertheless her father was exactly like mine. We talked every day comparing what our fathers said until she transferred to another school.

Many thanks to my son, Homer Jr., without whose assistance this book would not have been completed. Thank you for helping me to stay focused and to get my thoughts down on paper. I hope this book is entertaining and helpful to those who will read it.

Special thanks to my son-in-law Bob, for taking pictures of the statues and scanning them for the book. Bob helped to recover and save my manuscript when my computer crashed, not once but two times. Thank you Bob because I did not give you any rest until the book was completed.

Again, Thanks for a job well done.

Last but not least, this book is dedicated to my father, Charles Rudolph Rush, Sr. a legend in his own time. Daddy was always teaching, guiding, encouraging and demonstrating as he set examples for his six children. Although we feared him because of his strictness, he also received our utmost awe, love, and respect.

Daddy passed away in May of 1991 six years after we surprised him with a birthday party on his seventy-fifth birthday. We invited all his friends and former classmates. After thanking his guests and family he told everyone how proud he was of his children and our accomplishments. We all love him dearly and appreciate what we have learned from him as we have applied his wisdom in our lives every day. He taught his five girls and one son how to set goals and how to achieve those goals. "Believe in yourself and don't let anyone tell you what you can't do." These are the principles we used to accomplish success.

We are grateful for his love, encouragement, and guidance. Most of all, we thank him for keeping the family together after Mama passed. I truly believe he prepared us for the challenges and disappointments in life we have had and will encounter. We can overcome anything. We are also aware that life is not going to be a bed of roses.

Thank you, Daddy, for everything you taught us and all the things you said.

Introduction

Daddy was a legend in his own time. Bright, intelligent, and articulate, he was a man of particular savvy. Analytical and methodical, Daddy was a no-nonsense man. Yes, there might be other children who believe that their fathers were indeed legends in their own times as well. However, few could compare to *my father,* Charles Rudolph Rush Sr.

Having been given no middle name at birth, Daddy decided to add the name *Rudolph* later in life. Daddy did not complete high school; however, even though as a student he was both gifted and well advanced. Despite having only completed the tenth grade, he was quite capable of handling the challenges of my college assignments, much to my amazement. Daddy attended school in a one-room schoolhouse. He often told us how while learning his first grade lessons he would also listen to the teacher as she taught the second grade. The grades ran from first through the sixth. When he entered the second grade, he learned what the students were learning in the third grade. He told us he did this every year until he graduated from the sixth grade.

"Learn all you can," was one of his many mottos. He also stated "It doesn't matter how much 'book learning' you get! You've got to have common sense." Then he would give an example of someone he knew who, despite being highly intelligent, lacked common sense. I know today exactly what he was trying to teach us. Throughout my life's journey I have met a few highly intelligent people who had no "common sense" just as he explained to us.

Daddy was born in a little town in Jefferson County, Alabama. His family moved to West Virginia in a *hurry* because his father killed a white man, in self-defense. We were told our original last name was Pinkerton. Because of their hasty move, our last name was changed to Rush. Daddy tried all types of employment before he settled on being a brick mason. He worked in the coal mines in Bluefield. That job definitely was not for him. He told us about men getting trapped in the mines and never getting out. That's when he decided to do something else. He worked at Union Carbide in South Charleston, West Virginia. He worked in the steel mills in Pennsylvania. He told us about accidents happening in the mill when someone fell off the boardwalk. We would cover our faces as we pictured someone falling into the hot liquid. The melted steel was poured into beams. He also worked in the state of Ohio.

He was the best brick mason everywhere he was employed, truly a master of his craft. Every employer who had a son following in their footsteps wanted my father to teach their son the trade. Many supervisors' sons were apprentices of Daddy throughout his career.

Blackballed for his Beliefs

Daddy also looked out for others who tried to break into this trade. Making $15-$20 a day was a *lot* of money for a black man in those days. This was BIG money, as they would say back then. If one of his friends was not qualified as a brick mason, he would try to get them hired as a laborer. This job was mixing the mortar and bringing it on a hod to the brick mason. "Always reach back and help someone else whenever you can," he would tell us. That's exactly what he did. He helped many men to get employment. As a result of him trying to help other black men in this trade he was blackballed for many years in West Virginia.

Daddy began working in Ohio after he had written to the national union in Washington, D.C. He related the injustices the Negro bricklayers endured when seeking employment, specifically, being denied employment on government jobs. I wrote the letter he dictated. Lo and behold, he was contacted a week or so later. Two men came to Charleston and met with him. During that time, he was working on Diamond's Department Store project. (I would wave at him as I passed by coming from school.) After that meeting, at the union hall, several of the bricklayers were hired on the government jobs. However, Daddy was blackballed. He began working in Ohio. Of course, he contacted other bricklayers to come to Ohio when they couldn't get work. Several of the men rode along with him. He *always* looked out for others. One weekend, when Daddy and Uncle George were coming home from a job in Ohio, Uncle George had an accident.

At that time, there were no state highways, so everyone traveled over the mountains. Daddy told us that he would always follow behind the tractor trailer trucks. The drivers led them through the fog. Uncle George was in his car ahead of Daddy when his car rolled over and landed off the road. Uncle George was thrown out and pinned under his car. Daddy said there wasn't a soul around. He stopped his car and ran to help Uncle George. By this time, a trucker stopped. The trucker said he did not know how they would get Uncle George from beneath the car.

Daddy instructed the truck driver to pull him out as he lifted the car. Then he said, "Thelma, I don't know where my strength came from; God was with me. I grabbed the bumper and lifted that car way up in the air. It was as light as a feather". After the trucker dragged Uncle George from beneath the car, Daddy said he dropped the car fast. Miraculously, Uncle George was not seriously injured. He was sore for a while. Daddy was written up in the Charleston Gazette newspaper. There was a full-page write-up with his picture. The headline read "Superman Saves Brother." I guess the trucker told someone at the newspaper about this great feat. Later, Daddy told us that he would never be able to lift that car again even if someone offered him a million dollars.

The Brick Mason

Chapter 1

Daddy's Siblings

Daddy was close to his two brothers. Uncle Boob, Robert, was the eldest. Uncle George was the baby. Daddy was the middle child. However, he was always the one to take control of situations that happened in his mother's or the brothers' lives. I thought Daddy was the oldest for a long time until I learned differently. Daddy and Uncle Boob were tall in stature (over six feet tall.) Uncle George was short in stature. Uncle Boob entered my life when I was about eight or nine years old.

Uncle George lived three houses from ours. He had three boys: Joseph, George Henry and Charles Robert, whom we called Bobby. Uncle George's wife was Henrietta. She did not stay with him very long because Uncle George was very abusive. After a few years, Joseph, the oldest son left for the same reason. He joined the Army. For some reason I became his favorite cousin. We corresponded back and forth while he was in boot camp. When he came home on leave he brought me a watch. The fad then was streaking our hair with peroxide and wearing ankle bracelets. I was in the tenth grade. Wow, did Joe have a fit. I had never seen him so angry. He said only whores wore ankle bracelets and streaked their hair. When he finished his enlistment in the Army he never returned to Charleston. He married and settled in Roanoke, Virginia.

He had two sons. We corresponded for a couple of years. Though I never saw him again. He passed away many years ago.

Today Uncle George would have been called a "player" with a capital P. He ran off Aunt Henrietta because of his drinking and abuse. Every weekend was a battle for the women who moved in with him. After Aunt Henrietta left several women lived with him until they couldn't stand his abusive behavior. Miss Marjorie tried. She stood her ground for five or six years. Then she was out. Miss Betty was a feisty little woman in stature. They actually married and stayed together twenty some years. When word came that George Henry's helicopter was shot down in Vietnam, Uncle George became unbearable to live with. Miss Betty moved into the Washington Manor.

Uncle Boob lived uptown on Morris Street. He and Aunt Helen, his second wife, had a close relationship. I heard that his first wife, Ruth put him through the wringer. He had a daughter named Dorothy who was a deaf mute.

All the wives were very close. Frank Sinatra and his buddies were called the *Rat Pack*. Mama and the other wives were the female *Rat Pack*. On Sundays, if we did not go to St. Albans, they would get together at Uncle Boob's house. They usually met once or twice a month. What closeness these brothers and their wives shared. They never fell out with each other; never a cross word among them. This was quite unusual then watching today's reality shows featuring supposed best friends.

Chapter 2

Our Family

Mary Goldie

There are six siblings in my family—five girls and one boy (the baby). We were known throughout the neighborhood as the Rushes, the Rush girls, or Charlie Rush's daughters until Charles Jr. arrived.

Mary Goldie was the eldest. She was named after each grandmother. Mary was our paternal grandmother, and Golden was our maternal grandmother. However, my parents decided to name her Goldie instead of Golden. Mary Goldie is six years older than I am. She was Daddy's heart because she was the firstborn. Lovingly, he would call her his chocolate girl. Mary Goldie was beautiful. Her skin was smooth as silk. She had a keen nose and wore her hair in an upsweep with curls on top just like Lena Horne. She *loved* Lena Horne. She often wrote to her. One day she received a signed picture and a note from Ms. Horne. She was so excited and couldn't believe Lena Horne actually sent her a note and a signed photograph. Mary Goldie hung the picture on the wall in our bedroom.

Mary Goldie was gifted and talented. She could play anything on the piano, and she had a beautiful soprano voice. She won several trophies in business for being the fastest typist and taking dictation in shorthand. At Garnet High School, the only black high school and one of the best schools in Charleston, West Virginia, she excelled in business competitions. Garnet High was outstanding in business. Mary Goldie also played the cymbals in the band. Garnet's band traveled everywhere competing against other high school bands. Dr. Maude Wanzer Lange was a superb director. Every time the band left for a competition, there were more white folks at the train station cheering for them than black folks. *Everyone* was proud of Garnet High School's band. When Mary Goldie fell in love in the eleventh grade and married, she broke Daddy's heart. Daddy had so many hopes and dreams for his firstborn.

Although Mary Goldie was the firstborn she received her share of whippings. I recall when she received a well-deserved whipping. Mama and Daddy went out on one of their weekly dates. They were always home by ten o'clock. Mary Goldie was in charge. I was around seven or eight. Daddy had a drawer where he kept his gum, jewelry, money and important papers. We knew that we were not to touch that drawer. After Daddy and Mama left Mary Goldie opened the special drawer, took out all the gum (two packs) and began chewing all ten sticks. When she realized that all the gum was gone, she went back into Daddy's special drawer to get money to purchase more gum. "Here Zehline, you go to Skaff store and get some more Juicy Fruit gum". Well, to make a long story short (I was hit by a car while crossing the street.) I almost slid into the sewer. A white man jumped out of his car. As he was helping me up he kept asking if I was hurt. There was a lady with him. She kept insisting that they drive me home. I wouldn't let them. A crowd began to gather. The man kept asking if anyone knew this child. I hobbled home crying because I was in a lot of pain and frightened because I was not suppose to leave the house.

Mary Goldie didn't know what to do when she saw me. She began to panic when she saw her bedraggled injured sister. Mama and Daddy returned around ten o'clock. When they saw and heard me crying they asked, in unison, "What is wrong with Zehline?" I really started bawling as I related what Mary Goldie had done.I told them that she sent me to Skaff store on the corner. They didn't have any gum so I went to the second Skaff store on the next block. They were out of your brand of gum so I decided to go Joe Howard's grocery store. When I started crossing Court Street I was struck by the car. That's why Mary Goldie received her well-deserved whipping. She was always getting whippings.

Mama let me soak in warm water with Epsom Salt in the tub. By this time I had bruises on my lower body. I was so sore you could not touch me. After Daddy left for work each day Mama helped me to get into their bed. This was the routine everyday until I was able to be myself again. The next day after Daddy left for work there was a knock at the front door. It was the man who hit me the night before and the lady, his wife. They told Mama they asked someone in the crowd who I was and where I lived? They wanted to know how I was doing? The man apologized to me. Mama told them that I was bruised and sore. She was thankful I did not have any broken bones. The man gave Mama his name, address, telephone number and his insurance information. Before they left they told Mama to contact them if I needed anything, that their insurance would cover any medical bills. As I was writing about this incident I realized that these people were truly honest, caring and decent people. This was the character of the people when I was growing up.

As I grew older I believed Mary Goldie marched to a different drummer in life. She didn't listen even though she knew she would get chastised for her negative behavior. On another occasion Mama and Daddy went on their weekly date. Mary Goldie was instructed to not to let the baby chicks, just purchased, get wet. Mary Goldie was so engrossed playing the piano and singing, that when I tried to tell her that it was starting to rain she paid me no mind. And did it rain! The chicks were soaked! Mary Goldie brought the coop inside. She found a board to place over the bathtub. Then she found a cardboard box to put the chicks in. You will never guess what she did next! She turned on the oven and placed four or five chicks in the box to dry them off. After several minutes she would take them out then place another group of chicks into the oven. The little chicks were scurrying around because they were being cooked alive. Altogether there were twenty chicks. When Mama and Daddy returned home they inquired about the chicks. Did she bring them in before it started to rain? Mary Goldie was standing by the stove with a silly look on her face. For once I kept my mouth shut because of Daddy's facial expression. Then Daddy asked, "What was that noise?" Those chicks were really scurrying around. Daddy opened the oven door. "Mary Goldie what have you done?" She had to admit she let the chicks get wet. Daddy asked where the rest of the chicks were. She pointed to the bathroom. When Daddy entered the bathroom he hollered, "Thelma, come in here". Most of the chicks were lying on their backs with their little red legs and feet straight up in the air. Mary Goldie received her whipping. It would take another book to write about each of our misdeeds. We still laughed about this foolish action as we became adults.

February 11, 2007 3B

The Way It Was

By Richard Andre

Photo from Kanawha County Public Library

Court Street, 1955

SEGREGATION was on the ropes when this photo was taken, but the Triangle District was still a ghetto populated mostly by black citizens.

This scene at the north end of Court Street is typical of most of the Triangle District, which was originally one of the oldest white residential sections of Charleston. Many of the structures dated to the 19th century and were dilapidated, to say the least.

The district's name was derived from its shape on the map of Charleston, which encompassed the area generally bordered by the Elk River, the railroad, Washington Street and Capitol Street.

Interstate highway construction in the 1970s and projects like the water company brought an end to the Triangle District, and youngsters today have no idea where it was.

Richard, Andre (2007, February 11).
The Way It Was The Charleston Gazette, Section 3B

Zehline Ann

I am the second oldest. Named after our landlord's sister I was given the name Zehline. Mr. Hart and his sister were Syrians thus my name is Arabic. Until this day, I have sought to find the meaning of this name because I am constantly asked, "What does your name mean?" I was born on Easter eve. My mother informed the family I would not have a nickname such as Bunny. Thank you, Mama. To this day, all my siblings believe that I was Daddy's favorite.

Throughout the years, they have heard the story about how I survived when I was about seven months old. Daddy would tell us how one morning I was having trouble breathing. Mama started crying because my lips were turning blue. Daddy repeated what Mama said, "Come here, Charles, she's turning blue!" He demonstrated how I was gasping for breath. "I tore off all your clothes except your diaper, opened the door, and stuck you outside in the cold weather. When the cold air hit you, you began gasping short little gasps. Then you began crying." Every time he told us how he saved me, he would demonstrate, holding up his arms, cradling a baby, showing us how he did it. "You were crying, and Thelma was crying when I put you back into her arms." He was so proud whenever he told us about saving me. Many times we asked him, "How did you know what to do?" He would reply, "I didn't. It just came to me what to do." CPR had not been introduced back then. Daddy added as an afterthought, you never could keep any milk down. You were always throwing up". Unfortunately, I was always the one who was ill throughout my childhood. You name it. I had it.

Patricia Ester Elaine

Patricia Ester Elaine was born eighteen months later. She always wondered why she had three names when we all had two names. Ester was Mr. Hart's other sister. Daddy had great respect and a very good rapport with the Hart family, and the feeling was mutual.

Patricia's nickname is Tishy. She was very mischievous. She loved animals, gardening, and poultry. Daddy raised chickens in our backyard. Tishy had a name for each and every one of the hens. I don't remember her naming the roosters. There were two of them. She even tried to raise a duck. Kitty Yellow was her cat's name. The one pet that our parents refused to allow her to have was a dog. Tishy knew that I was afraid of *everything*, even my shadow. She would tease me by holding a chicken close to my face saying, "It's going to get you." Another time, she was holding Kitty Yellow, the cat, teasing me again. As I ran to tell Mama, she had the nerve to throw that cat on my back. You never heard such hollering and screaming in your life.

Patricia loved to grow flowers and vegetables. She and Mama had a garden in Uncle George's back yard. Tishy would get her red wagon and gardening tools ready and they would head to Uncle George's backyard. Once in a while I would watch them work in the garden. They grew green beans, corn and tomatoes as I recall. Everything was going nicely until Tishy became tired of getting the broom and sweeping the yard and the dirt off the slate stones leading up to our side door. She decided that we should have grass just like Uncle George. She began taking squares of sod from his yard and planting it in our yard. She was discreet in the beginning. Then she became a little eager to have her own grass. At first she was taking the sod from places Uncle George would not notice. Then she decided to take enough sod to cover the whole side of our yard. One evening Uncle George came down the street screaming at the top of his lungs, "Where is Patricia?" She has ruined my yard!" Tishy tried to looked as if she was innocent when he shouted in her face that she better not come in his yard again. I don't recall if Daddy disciplined her with a whipping. Thanks to Patricia we finally had grass. Later on we planted grass in the front yard.

Today we laugh a lot about the *good ole days* especially about the summer we went to visit with our paternal grandmother Nina. Nina married a minister after Daddy's father was killed in the coal mines. They lived in Bluefield, West Virginia. They moved a lot. Anyway, one Sunday on the way to church, we were dressed in beautiful white dresses Mama made. Mama dressed us as twins: people *thought* we were twins. It was a really hot day riding in the car with all the windows down and we were in the backseat. Patricia decided to take several sticks of gum from the special candy dish Nina had. Every evening, we were allowed to select a piece of candy from that beautiful crystal dish. Tishy, unknown to us, chewed several sticks of gum as we were riding along to church. When we arrived at the church, our dresses were covered with strings of chewing gum. Strings of gum went from the roof of the car across the backseat. The back of the car looked like it had spider webs hanging everywhere. Nina was furious as she tried to remove the gum using ice cubes. That Sunday we sat in the back of the church.

From left to right Ramona, Patricia, Mary Goldie and Zehline

When we became adults, Tishy admitted that she was jealous because I received so much attention from everyone. I said, "You knew that I was always ill. I couldn't help being ill all the time." She told me that she realized this when she became an adult. She said, "When you are a child, you do not think logically. All I wanted was the same attention". Today we are all very close. She and her husband moved from Nevada to be near Monie and me in Atlanta, for two years before returning to West Virginia. We talk all the time on the telephone, and Monie and I visit her frequently.

Ramona Jean

Ramona Jean, Monie, made her entrance into the Rush family three years after Tishy. She loved to throw fits. Whenever things did not go her way, she would drop to the floor, roll around, and holler. Don't ask me why but for some reason I decided to be her buffer from spankings. I thought she was so cute. Whenever she required a spanking, I would intervene, saying to Mama, "Don't whip her. She's too cute to get a whipping". Mama's response was, "If you think she is so cute, then you take her whippings." I did for quite some time because Monie was also devious and mischievous.

One day while I was taking *her* punishment she started laughing. That was the last day I took her punishments. When we get together, reminiscing, Monie would say, all the while laughing, "I made a big mistake by laughing. And I cried whenever you took my punishments".

But this one time, Monie said I looked like a chicken with its head wrung off. We always received our punishment on our legs with switches. As we became older, we had to pick our own switches. Oh Lord, don't get skimpy ones that would snap after a few whacks. Then we were in *big* trouble. We often laugh about this even today.

One Christmas, we all hid her toys and presents. We replaced them with bunches of switches tied with a big red bow around them (Tishy's idea). Monie's face fell when she entered the living room, and Tishy told her, "This is what Santa left you because you weren't good at all this year." Monie immediately dropped to the floor, screaming and hollering. Mama called us into the kitchen (she was angry). She told us that she was taking Monie to visit Aunt Betty and Uncle George, and we better have Monie's things back under the tree when they returned home. Uncle George and Miss Betty (that's what we called her) lived three doors from our house. Monie and Mama returned to the house fifteen or twenty minutes later. Monie ran excitedly into the living room to see all her gifts and toys. We all acted excited and surprised. We said, "Look what Santa brought you!" Tishy said, "He decided to give you a second chance." How about that, the pot talking to the kettle? Monie didn't pay any attention to us because she was too busy opening her gifts and playing with her toys.

Suzette Denise

Suzette made her debut five years after Monie. She is the baby girl. She does not have a nickname. However, I sometimes call her Susie Baby. I recall hearing Daddy say to Mama "I guess we will keep trying until we get a boy". However, he was delighted to have another girl. I believe he was the one to give her the name Suzette. Mama added Denise.

Suzette loved to dance. She knew all the latest dancing crazes. She especially loved to show us how to do the "Monkey." She was very quiet and shy until she became a teenager. After Mama passed on, I wasn't around much. I married and traveled with Homer in the military. Suzette was in the second grade. Now Tishy was in charge.

Another tragedy happened in Suzette's life while she was in college, West Virginia State of course. She was in her second year when she and her boyfriend William (Billy) James decided to marry. He was drafted in February. They already had a son. The marriage took place on March 9, 1969. They were so happy. Shortly after the marriage Billy chose to go into the Marines. He went to boot camp. After his six week stint he came home for three weeks. Then he was off to California. After a month he was shipped off to Vietnam. Eight months into the marriage Suzette had a visit from two military officers. The news no one ever wants to receive: "We are sorry to tell you that your husband has been killed in the line of duty." Billy had been killed on November 19, 1969 and Suzette was notified two weeks later.

Daddy was there for her and Jeffrey. The baby was truly a blessing for both of them. Daddy was crazy about Jeffrey. Suzette was encouraged to continue her education. She graduated with a BS in Sociology. Today, Suzette has been blessed with another son. His name is Tony.

Charles Rudolph Jr.

Finally, finally, finally, a boy arrived. We were all so happy when Charles arrived! Although Charles was the only boy and the baby, I must admit he wasn't spoiled. He was a typical boy. Charles played on the little league baseball team. While he was in high school and college, he excelled in the sport of basketball. He is handsome. Lots of girls were constantly seeking his attention. Unfortunately, Mama passed away when he was in the first grade. That's when Daddy told me that I would be in charge (handling the finances) until I left home. Then the next one in line would take over. "We are going to stay a family," Daddy told us. Our maternal grandmother, Gogo, came to live with us, along with our Aunt Marie. I was in college and married; Homer was in Wyoming, training in boot camp. He joined the Air Force. Tishy was in high school. Monie was in junior high. Suzette and Charles were in elementary school.

Charles went on to graduate from West Virginia State College also. He married and became a parole officer in Ohio.

Chapter 3

Religious Experiences

Every Sunday, we had a dynamite breakfast before going to Sunday school. Mama would have fried apples, thick slabs of bacon, *Gunnoed* sausages, scrambled eggs, and homemade biscuits. The biscuits were fluffy, high, light, and melted in our mouths.

My Mama could really cook. None of us can come close to her cooking. We all can cook or as the saying goes we can all "throw down" in the kitchen, yet none of us can cook like Mama. I later learned how to make light rolls (almost like hers). Ramona can make delicious cakes, close to hers, and Patricia can make pies. All three of us can duplicate her potato salad. After eating our delicious breakfast off we went to Sunday school dressed in our Sunday best made by Mama.

When we were younger, Daddy drove us to Sunday school. At eleven o'clock, our parents arrived for Sunday services. They sat up front. We sat in the center pews near the back. Sometimes we sat on the right-hand side near the stained glass windows when we were not singing in the choir. In the evening we returned to church for Catechism, and every Wednesday we went to choir practice. We always walked home with our friends.

Both of our parents were very active in the church, Daddy was the head trustee and Mama was the secretary of the Parsonage Club and a member of the H and L Club.

Daddy was an active member of St. Paul AME Church for fifty-five years until his health began to fail. He helped to build St. Paul AME Church at the Court Street site. He also helped with the construction of the present church on Second Avenue on the West Side.

Chapter 4

Bible Stories

If you wanted to know any thing about history or the Bible, Daddy was the one to ask. "If you read the Bible about wars, we all could learn how history repeats itself. "Maybe we could prevent wars if our leaders studied wars in the Bible." Our government should take care of its own affairs before we go to other countries telling them what they should be doing and how to run their country". Jokingly, he would say, "It would be something if the two leaders of warring countries fought it out: boxing or some other way. This would eliminate our boys losing their lives. The winner would be announced to the world. That would be it. Of course, it would never happen this way," he would say laughing.

Daddy would tell us stories from the Bible. We loved listening about Adam and Eve's disobedience to God. He explained why they were driven out of the Garden of Eden. They'd had a perfect life. "Eve never should have listened to that snake'. They had everything they needed and yet they disobeyed God. That's why we have choices today. "We have to make the decision to live as a good or bad person". "The lesson from this story: When you make wrong choices you must suffer the consequences. In other words, You can make your bed hard or you can make it soft; either way you have to lie on it".

We listened to stories about Noah and the Ark. The peoples' negative behavior caused God to destroy the Earth. Some of the other stories were about David and Goliath, Samson and Delilah. Samson lost all his strength because he revealed to Delilah his strength was in the length of his hair. Joshua led the Israelites to march around the walls of Jericho until the walls fell down. The Israelites were small in number, but the enemy was not aware of this. The Israelites believed Joshua and his men were a mighty army. They won because Joshua listened to God. At one time everyone spoke the same language until the people decided to build a tower to reach the sky. This story is called the *Tower of Babel*. Cain was so jealous of his brother, Abel, he decided to kill him. This was the first murder in history. Jonah was swallowed into the belly of a whale. Moses led his people out of bondage from Egypt and the Pharaoh. We always sat quietly listening in awe as he spoke.

Chapter 5

Celebrating Holidays

Christmas

Every Christmas was a wonderful and happy time in the Rush household. We were all excited as we were given our shopping money for gifts. We would go shopping every Saturday in December to purchase gifts for each other and Mama and Daddy. I loved going to Woolworth's, Kresege's, Lerner's, and McCrory department stores. I can still smell the perfume that was in a deep blue colored bottle shaped like a heart. I never purchased it because I did not like its smell but every year I admired how it was so beautifully packaged for the holiday. It was so much fun listening to the Christmas carols as we shopped. I also enjoyed shopping in JC Penny, Stone and Thomas, and Diamonds. These were "the" department stores. As I grew older these were the department stores where I continued to shop.

When we were old enough to work we all started working and doing the same as Daddy, saving our money. Faithfully, daddy would open a Christmas Club the week after Christmas. I followed this practice as well and continued doing so even after I was married. Later Christmas Clubs became unpopular with banks. When I became a teacher the credit union where

I was a member offered a Christmas Saving Club as well as a Summer Club. Because teachers did not receive pay during the summer months, teachers either saved a portion of their weekly pay in the Summer Club to cover the three months without pay or went into debt borrowing enough to carry them through the summer months.

Daddy would take all five girls and later all six of us (once our baby brother was born) to shop for a Christmas tree. It would be cold and snowy. I didn't care much about selecting a tree because I did not like being in the cold. As I grew older most of the time I waited at home until they returned. On the other hand, Mary Goldie and Tishy's excitement could not be contained. They usually selected the tree and watched as Daddy and the seller known to us as the "Christmas Tree Man" tied the tree to the top of our car.

Now, I liked getting the decorations ready. We would put on the Christmas music and decorate the tree. Oh, it was a joyous occasion! First, we would put on the lights. Some years we would decorate with only one color of bulbs and lights. Other years we would have multi-colored bulbs and lights. We would turn the lights on. Next, we put on the bulbs. There was a special bulb for each of us. Later, during the years we purchased the blinking lights. It was something to put the angel on the top! The final touch was the angel hair. Then we would just sit and gaze at our handy work scratching as angel hair made us itch.

We had so much fun wrapping the gifts for one another. We would tell each other there was no peeking. Mama would be in the kitchen baking, baking, baking cookies, cakes, pies. I always helped make the cookies for Santa. They were sugar cookies. I would sprinkle the red and green sugar on them. Then we would place a plate of cookies on the kitchen table with a glass of milk for Santa. Mama would tell us we had to go to bed because Santa would not come until we were fast asleep. It was sooo hard to go to sleep. It was always after midnight when we would finally climb into bed. Daddy would always go out after supper and return at eleven o'clock. He would tell us the story "T'was the Night Before Christmas". We always waited up to hear him tell this story. No matter how many times we heard it. We loved it when he talked as if he were Santa talking to his reindeer. Later, when we were older and would be sitting around talking about Christmas, Daddy would describe how wide eyed we looked when we saw what Santa brought us.

Easter

Easter was another one of our favorite holidays. When we were younger Daddy always told us about the Easter Bunny and Peter Cottontail. There was a song he would sing to us which went, "Here comes Peter Cottontail, hopping down the bunny's trail, hippity, hoppity Easter's on its way".

Mama would take us shopping for our socks, shoes, hats, and gloves. As you already know, Mama made all of our outfits. She would stay up all night getting our outfits ready. We were busy in the kitchen dying eggs and wondering about the Easter baskets we would get. Daddy always reminded us of the real reason for celebrating Easter. He told us that man made this holiday and Christmas for commercial reasons. "It is their way of cashing in and making money." "Just remember Christ's birth and death." "He came to save mankind and died for our sins."

The Crucifion

Chapter 6

Family Time
Listening to the Radio

Every evening, we all gathered around the radio in Mama and Daddy's bedroom. We would listen to the *Shadow, Stella Dallas*, and *Inner Sanctum*. On Saturdays, we listened to the *Hit Parade* and Frank Sinatra. Saturday mornings we listened to *Radio City, Time Square, Johnny Mack Brown, Sergeant Preston of the Yukon*, and the *Lone Ranger* as we cleaned the house from the front to the back singing "Happy Trails to You" along with Roy Rogers and Dale Evans. I loved the Grand Central Station's stories. Every week there was a new story about a passenger riding the train into the station. How we used our imagination visualizing every word the narrator spoke! As the train rolled into the station the whistle was blowing. Next, you could hear the wheels screeching on the tracks as the train stopped. Then you would hear the hissing sound of the steam blowing out of the stack. The train had arrived into the station. The narrator began telling the story. He revealed information about one passenger as he or she left the train. Next he would tell why this passenger rode the train into New York. The commercials were great! We heard jingles: "Trixs are for kids," "Cream of Wheat is so good to eat. We have it every day." "Hot Ovaltine, hot Ovaltine, that's the way to start the day!" I sang along with the commercials as I cleaned the house.

After we cleaned the house inside and outside, we went to the Ferguson's Theater on the Block. That's what that part of town was called. Every Saturday, there was a serial; the *Zombie's Curse* or the *Purple Monster*. We did not want to miss a single one. The newsreel came on first showing the events happening in the world. The events happened a week or two previously. Not today, we see the wars instantly every night in our homes through television and on the Internet.

After the movie, we stopped in at the M&S Drug Store to get ice cream or a hot dog. (Two African American pharmacists were the owners Dr. Mitchell and Dr. Saul.) That ice cream was *so* delicious! Today it's not made the way it was made back then. Then it was made of pure milk without all the added preservatives in ice cream today. Our mouths watered as our Aunt Mildred scooped each dip onto the cone. She would tell us to hurry up and get out of there after we paid for our ice cream. We walked in a group, including Carl King. We had to pass all the men hanging out on the corners of Washington and Shrewsbury Streets. M&S Drug Store was on this corner. They would holler and whistle at the girls passing by. "Hey, Miss Fine" and other things. For a long time we were forbidden to go into the drugstore before our Aunt began working there. The men and older boys hung out on the corner of Washington and Shrewsbury Streets making it difficult to walk by them. When we walked by, the men parted like the Red Sea. We could hear them say, "Don't mess with those girls. "Those girls are Charlie Rush's daughters". You don't mess with them!" No one ever made catcalls after us. It was quiet until we passed through the line of men.

We (Patricia and I) could go to the shoe shop on Court Street together if we needed to have our shoes repaired. We usually went on Saturday mornings. One particular Saturday morning, we were on our way to the shoe shop. I was surprised that the men on Court Street also knew not to mess with Charlie Rush's daughters.

We passed three men. Two of them made like it was a big deal to get out of our way. One of them said, "Uh, uh, uh, look at this!" The other man grabbed his arm, hissing in his ear, "Those girls are Charlie Rush's daughters". "Oh yeah," they said sheepishly as they slinked away. I must say that our father was one powerful (don't mess with his daughters) influential man. When he let the men know *Don't Mess with his Daughters* that's exactly what he meant.

Daddy said, "Boys and men will treat you the way you carry yourself. If you are loose, acting wild and giggling at everything they say, they won't respect you. Carry yourself so they won't have any reason to disrespect you. I'm out here every night and I see some of these girls (some are your classmates) out in the street, letting men pull and paw all over them and they are grinning and giggling, hee hee hee" He did not believe girls should be out in the streets.

Chapter 7

Fun Times with Daddy

Daddy had stacks and stacks of long playing (LP) records of all the famous musicians: Duke Ellington, Cab Callaway, Count Basie, Billy Eckstein, Louie Armstrong, Billie Holiday, and Artie Shaw. We had a floor model Victrola in our living room. Sometimes we would put on a record and begin dancing. Daddy always joined in saying, "You girls don't know how to dance." Then he would grab Mama's hand, "Come on Thelma, let's show them how to dance." They always began with *Swing* or the *Jive*. Eventually they ended up dancing the *Lindy Hop*. That's when we would say "Ugh, that's old timey." Daddy would fall out laughing. He would say to Mama, "We showed them, Thelma, how to dance." Those were the good ole days!

Mary Goldie, Patricia and I took piano lessons from Dr. Maude Wanzer Lange. Mary Goldie could play every piece of music perfectly and beautifully. I learned to read the notes well but not as well as Mary Goldie. Patricia struggled because she wasn't really into playing the piano.

Once a week we went for piano lessons at Dr. Lange's home. One day Dr. Lange discovered that Mary Goldie could not read music. She played by ear. Mary Goldie would have Janet King, Carl's older sister, to play her lessons (*one time*) then she would play it perfectly. (Carl was my best friend.) Dr. Lange would be in another room listening when we played. She kept asking Mary Goldie to play a certain passage. She would start from the beginning of the selection. Finally, Dr. Lange returned to the room and pointed to what she wanted her to play. She continued to start from the beginning of the selection. Mary Goldie finally confessed that Janet King, who was an excellent pianist, played her lessons for her. Then she would play it exactly as Janet played them. Daddy could not believe it until he gave Mary Goldie a selection to play. She couldn't play it. He sent one of us to get Janet. She played the selection once then Mary Goldie played it perfectly. Daddy said, "Well I'll be doggone!"

We practiced one hour every day after school. *Miss Goody Two Shoes*, the name Patricia gave me, ran to practice first. Then I would go outside to play with my friends. One day Patricia out smarted herself. Many times Mama would say to her, "That was the fastest hour of practicing, Patricia." Tishy would play five or ten minutes stop advance the minute hand on the clock ten or fifteen minutes. She continued doing this until she had advanced the hand to the next hour. Well, Miss Patricia forgot to set the clock back one day. When Daddy returned home from work he was livid. He began bellowing the minute he walked through the gate. "Where is Patricia?" He was on the job one hour early. He always left at five o'clock. No one was there when he arrived. He knew it was Patricia who "messed with the clock. Wow, I thought, it's funny how Mama and Daddy knew which child did a misdeed.

Tishy loved to dance. Daddy decided to sign her up to take tap dancing lessons. She would come home after her lessons and demonstrate what she learned. She really shined when she was in a recital. Daddy was proud of her accomplishment.

Every year a show, *Silas Green from New Orleans* came to town. It was a show with comedians, singers and dancers. One year Tishy was invited to come on the stage to dance. That was a big mistake. Tishy was in *seventh* heaven. She danced her heart out.

The more the audience clapped, the more she danced. Daddy had to coax her off the stage.

Every Sunday I was paid to play the piano for Sunday School. One Sunday I was ill. Mr. Wooster, the Superintendent, asked Tishy to play. She informed him that she couldn't play the piano. After Mr. Wooster told her that all the Rush girls could play the piano she said, "Okay." She told us that she started playing the first three or four bars of the song. Then she began banging, plink, plonk, bang, plink plonk, banging up and down the keyboard. Everyone stopped singing. Tishy told us that everyone was looking at her: the adults and the children. She turned around on the piano stool and held her hand out to Mr. Wooster. She asked, "Where's my money?" Mr. Wooster laughed and told her she would get her money. Daddy said, "Patricia, you know better than that." "Well, I told him that I could not play the piano. When I told him that, he insisted that I could play. So I deserved the money". Daddy just shook his head with a small smile on his face.

After Dr. Lange passed I continued to take lessons from John Randolph. Daddy beamed when I played a duet with Mr. Randolph every year until I entered college.

Roller Skating

Every Friday we piled into the car to visit with the Faulkner family, our cousins on Mama's side of the family. Mama always remained behind to visit with her cousin Ellen and her husband Joe while we went to the skating rink. Daddy was a very good skater and instructor. Sometimes Daddy would invite Carl King to come with us. Carl learned how to skate much quicker than we did. You already know why I learned to skate very quickly.

The first time we went to the rink, all of us had a difficult time staying upright on our skates. Daddy would take turns teaching each one of us how to skate, especially when we came to the corners. As he took each one of us around the rink, he would say, "Yes, you are going to fall down until you get the hang of it. Everything seems hard until you keep at it; until you accomplish it". Then he would say, "Get out there and roll." "When you fall get up and keep trying until you get it accomplished." Our first encounter with learning to skate left us with sore rear ends and bruises from bouncing off the floor and flying into the side rails. Tishy commented that she was surprised that I had not broken any bones because I didn't have much "meat" on my bones to bounce on.

Many times Daddy would take Patricia and me when he would wash his car in a little creek in the country. He always said to us, "Let me take my girls to the country so they can see some cows, horses, and chickens". We already knew how live chickens looked because we raised them. Skaff store on the corner sold live chickens. The chickens were crowded together in coops. Customers would select one or two chickens. Maxine or her brother Paul would wring their necks, scald the feathers off them, and then weigh them for the customer. It was years before I would eat chicken after seeing how the chicken arrived on our dinner table.

We also raised chickens. They were Patricia's pets. That was another reason why I did not eat a lot of chicken growing up. Mama always waited until we left for Sunday school, then she would kill a chicken for dinner. When Tishy returned home she counted the chickens. Next we would hear her hollering and screaming, "You killed Sally" or you killed Penny." Ugh! I did not want to eat a pet chicken.

As I mentioned before Daddy would take Patricia (Tishy) and me with him whenever he washed his car. I remember our outfits were white with pink-trimmed ruffled cap sleeves. Mama made all our clothes. People thought we were twins for years. That was until I grew older and did not want anyone to have the same clothes as mine. As I recall, we would drive to the country and Daddy would park the car in a little stream. We were instructed to play on the bank covered with lots of white cold sand. Each time I recall this part of our life, I can still feel the cool breeze flowing across my body. Tishy and I started to build sand castles with our pails and shovels. As always, mischievous Tishy was up to no good. After meticulously building my own sand castle, Tishy stood up, walked over to mine, and knocked it down. Daddy always had to chastise her for her negative behavior. Daddy continued to drill home the benefits of family unity and treating one another the way you would like to be treated. In fact he always told us to think about how you would want to be treated before we say or do something to someone. Would you want to be on the receiving end of what you are going to say or do?

Window Shopping

We all had lots of clothes and shoes. We had so many clothes Daddy had to partition a corner of our bedroom and build a closet. The four of us had so many skirts and sweaters; the clothes were taking over the room.

On Sundays, Daddy and Mama would take us downtown to window-shop. We all ran to look at the clothes. Daddy told us, "I have never seen girls like you in my life. You always ran to look at the clothes, never the toys." As we became older, we all had little paying jobs. We learned from our father, of course, how to use layaway for the clothes we wanted. That's another reason why he had to build a closet. Clothes, clothes, clothes, that is all we ever wanted. Yes, we all love our clothes. "Always look your best when you leave the house;" another one of Daddy's quotes.

The Neighborhood Children

Many times, Daddy would take a few of the neighborhood children on outings. He would drive to the county line then turn around. On the way home, we stopped to get ice cream cones. My friend, Carl King, would fondly recall these outings whenever we would get together. He told me that was the only time he ever got an ice cream cone. Carl would say, "Your father would pile up his car with the neighborhood kids, as many of us who could get into that car." He added, "Of course, you always sat in the front seat." We had so much fun! The children who were left behind made sure they would go the next time.

Weekly Neighborhood Lessons

Daddy loved spelling bees, math and geography reviews. Each week he held a review with all the neighborhood kids. Everyone always gathered in our front yard. I guess that is why I am so competitive. That's because I certainly wasn't letting any of my friends outshine me in my yard and in front of my father. Every week we eagerly waited to tell Daddy how much we had learned during the week. These reviews really kept us all on our toes, especially me; I did not want to fail. My father was testing us.

I was very shy (afraid of my shadow). My family encouraged me to overcome my shyness. I had to overcome shyness because Carl was the one we had to watch. He was very bright and very good with math. Even today, when I recall those weekly reviews I can see Carl's face beaming whenever Daddy praised and encouraged him to always do his best. Before his death, we would reminisce about the good ole days every time he telephoned or visited. I was a grade ahead of him. We would talk and he would remind me of how I would teach him what I had learned in school each day. Then he'd say, "I'll be doggone, you did become a teacher. I was ahead of the other children when I started school because of your teaching." My friend passed away in June 2004. We were always in friendly competition against each other. Carl was truly a good friend. I really miss him.

Sometimes when Daddy returned from work he would stop and watch me teaching some of the neighborhood kids. (We all had to be in the yard upon his arrival at 4:30). I never have forgotten his remarks to me until this day! Although he said it jokingly, I did not take it as a joke. He said, "You are going to be an old maid schoolteacher." That bothered me because I was so thin and bony. Tishy called me "bacon feet" because I wore 4A width shoes. I couldn't sit on Mama's lap very long because my bones would *cut* her. Anyway, Daddy was partially correct. I did become a teacher but also married. As for the shyness I had, not anymore! People I know today do not believe me when I tell them how shy I was growing up. Maybe that could be why Daddy had those weekly reviews.

At 4:30 sharp, we were in the yard or on the front porch upon Daddy's arrival from work. After Daddy taught us how to skate Patricia, Carl and I would skate all day on McCormick Street during the summer until dinnertime. While Daddy was taking his bath we helped Mama set the table. Everyday we ate at the kitchen table in that little kitchen. We shared what we had done during the day. Those were the good ole days! Mama cooked everything from scratch. The meals were so delicious!

Every Friday night we waited for Daddy to bring ice cream. The ice cream was *Valley Bell*, the most delicious ice cream you could ever eat. Daddy would always purchase our favorite flavors; mine was butter pecan. Each one of us received a half of a pint. Mama would split the pint in half for each of us. We watched eagerly as she took a knife and split the pint in half. We were allowed to stay up late and watch television because it was the weekend.

Chapter 8

The Importance of Reading

Reading was Daddy's top priority. He read a lot about *everything*. He was a self-made man. He read books on how to lay brick. How about that? This is why I followed in his footsteps; reading. We had to read, read and read. I love reading. We went to the library at school every week. During the summer, we registered for the summer reading program. One year I won a prize for reading the most books. Daddy was so proud of my accomplishment. I thought the certificate was something. I did not care about the prize. In fact, I don't recall what it was, probably a book. "You can travel anywhere in the world through books," was another one of Daddy's favorite sayings.

Later, when I married my high school sweetheart, Homer I was able to visit some of the places I had read about. Because Homer enlisted in the United States Air Force I was able to travel throughout the States and Europe. I was in awe wherever he was stationed in the States or a foreign Country because I actually was seeing places I had read about growing up. We lived in South Dakota, Indiana, Massachusetts and Italy. I was elected the president of the Protestant Women of the Chapel. I traveled throughout Italy and Germany speaking on the behalf of Protestant Women of the Chapel, PWOC. As we traveled from place to place I was thrilled because I could not believe I was seeing everything I had read about. Seeing the basilicas and the tombs underground, the Spanish Steps, the Statue of David, the Leaning Tower of Pisa, the Trevi Fountain, the opera house in Verona, St. Peters' Square, and the Coliseum were amazing! Riding in a gondola and being serenaded was unbelievable. The most remarkable memory was an audience with the Pope.

The Protestant Women of the Chapel's (PWOC) publicity department sent a news article about my travels representing them after the annual meeting at Berchtesgaden, Germany. The information was sent to the Gazette newspaper in my hometown. One day a letter arrived from Miss Gamble, my first grade teacher stating that she always knew I would do something to be proud of. She stated how proud she was of my accomplishments. I was truly surprised and touched. Wow! My first grade teacher writing to me reminded me how I felt in her room whenever she praised me about something I had accomplished.

Daddy always told us that we were fortunate to be able to visit the places I had read about. While I was in Italy I would call him sometimes to tell him about my adventures. One day I probably will write another book about my experiences being a military wife.

We were encouraged to enter contests. This is one of my hobbies still today. I recall winning an essay contest sponsored by a local radio station. Carl's father helped me organize my thoughts and edited the essay. I wrote an essay about David from the Bible: how he used music to soothe the savage beast as an example in the essay. I was amazed when I received a letter notifying me I had won second place. I ran to Carl's house to show the letter to Mr. King. He told me that I was a bright little girl and to keep up the good work. I beamed like the sun as he patted me on the head.

Carl King was my best friend from the day his family moved into our neighborhood. I believe they moved from Welch, West Virginia. When we entered high school he and Homer, my future husband at that time, became best of friends forever. They did everything together. Another time I won count-the-jelly beans contest. Every year Kresge's department store had a display for the Easter holiday. There were live bunnies in the window also. I walked the length of the window several times counting those jellybeans. I was determined that I could count the exact number of jellybeans. Again I was surprised when I was notified that I was the winner a few days before Easter.

Chapter 9

Our School Days

Elementary School

We all attended Booker T. Washington School. The school was a stone's throw from our house: just around the corner. Sometimes we climbed over the back fence for a short cut. We came home for lunch to some very wholesome, delicious lunches. Occasionally we ate at school. I was five years old when I entered the first grade. I loved school! Every teacher influenced my life today. We had wonderful, caring, no-nonsense teachers. Ms. Gamble was my first-grade teacher. It was like magic, learning to read books. The reader was *Dick and Jane.* They had a pet dog named Spot. I was beaming from ear to ear when I was able to read the entire reader to Daddy.

We had an instrumental band. Every week we learned to play a different instrument. On Wednesdays, twice a month, we listened to a classical music program on the radio. Then we would have an art lesson, drawing what you visualized as the music was played again. I would draw my heart out because I wanted my work to be displayed in the entrance hallway.

Mrs. Bennett was my third-grade teacher on the first floor. She was a very good teacher also. However, I wanted to get to the second floor. That's where the "mature" students were: grades four through six.

Mrs. Dorothy Hubbard was my fourth-grade teacher. I was in love with her. She shared her personal life with us. She was always telling us about her daughter Peggy. Mrs. Hubbard was so proud of her. She would tell us how and what she was doing in college. Everyone respected her. She would leave the room (for hours, it seemed like it), and no one talked nor moved out of his or her seat. She brought out the creative nature in us.

Once I wrote a play. She thought it was fantastic! I was surprised when she asked me to present the play. Some of the children were selected to play parts. Others were selected to make the scenery and costumes. I was proud as a peacock as I delegated my classmates to each task. Why? It was because I was *very* shy. Everyone was excited and cooperative. My confidence in myself began to soar.

Mrs. Laura Pounds was my fifth-grade teacher. She loved music and paintings. She played the piano. We sang, *Santa Lucia* her favorite song every day. We studied famous painters. I recall the painting of the *Blue Boy* placed on the wall above the chalkboard. I really like the artwork of Van Gogh and Monet. Mrs. Pounds was a happy teacher, very cheerful, with sparkling eyes and long black hair. She was a stickler when it came to math and English.

One day the sparkle went out of her eyes. Mrs. Pounds' husband was a firefighter. It was around one o'clock or two o'clock when Mr. Carpenter, the principal, entered our room. He told Mrs. Pounds, in a hushed voice in the corner of the room, that Woolworth Five and Dime store was on fire. The fire was horrific! We were all very quiet the rest of the day because we saw how upset Mrs. Pounds was. Before school was over, we learned that several firemen had fallen through the second floor. Mrs. Pounds' husband was one of these firemen. (Even today I recall how those wooden floor looked on the second and third floors. They were rough sawed wide planks.) Mrs. Pounds crumble like a limp rag into her chair. She made it through the day because it was dismissal time. She was never the same Mrs. Pounds I knew from the first day I entered her classroom. We did not see her again until a few weeks before school was out. She tried to be upbeat but things were different. I felt useless helpless because I did not know how to help her with her pain. I wanted it to go away. Even today, when I think back on that day, I don't know how she did it. She is still one of my favorites to this day.

Mr. Carpenter, the principal was also my sixth-grade teacher. No one wanted to be sent to his office for discipline. Corporal punishment was not considered to be abusive in those days. As we were told by our parents, "If you ever are sent to the principal's office, expect the same thing you received there, waiting for you when you get home". This message was true for *every* grade: Stay out of trouble, learn your lessons, and do your best. Students who did go to Mr. Carpenter's office received three whacks with a wide strap on their derriere. Girls received three whacks in the palm of their hand. Whenever a classmate was sent to his office, we labeled them as "bad." Some of them would brag about it, but they didn't really mean it. It was their way of covering up their embarrassment. Mr. Carpenter was a kind, gentle man. His teaching strengths were math, grammar, and history. Everyone loved him (even the 'bad behavior' ones).

Junior High

In the fall I entered the seventh grade at Boyd Junior High School. Boy, was I excited! I was eleven years old. Mr. Callaway was the principal. He also attended my church, St. Paul AME Church. Guess what? Some of the teachers went to school with my father. They all spoke highly of him. There was Mr. Reuben (printing and civic), Mr. Goff (math), Mr. Napier (algebra and PE) Mrs. Jennings (science and home economics), Mrs. Winston (math), and Mrs. Carter (English and literature). She loved *Silas Marner*. I still remember the book today.

Another teacher was Mrs. Printess (geography and history). I loved her history classes because I loved learning about *our* history. (I guess it is because Daddy loved history.) Miss Gravely taught physical education and health. All of my teachers taught two subjects. I can't remember the other subject Mrs. Winston taught.

We walked eight blocks to school in the rain, sleet or snow every day as we watched the buses pass by us with the white children. We also passed by their school and watched them get off their buses. You know it never bothered us. We were physically fit; fit as fiddles from walking. Sometimes we walked the back way to school passing Garnet High School. *That* was our ultimate goal. We all wanted to follow in Mary Goldie's footsteps. We wanted to go to Garnet High School too.

In junior high school, I didn't follow the norm. I took printing. I loved doing typesetting. Mr. Rueben was the teacher. Wouldn't you know it? He knew Daddy very well. In fact, I learned that most of the teachers at Boyd Junior High either went to school with him or knew him from some other means. All of my teachers were GREAT! Some were harder on me than others. At that time I did not appreciate being *leaned* on by a few of them. However, I appreciated it later in life because they *really* cared about me reaching my potential.

Because most of the teachers knew my father, I *had* to stay on my toes, dot my *i*'s and cross my *t*'s. I really had to apply myself, especially in general math and algebra. I worked really hard to get a B. I remember telling Daddy that I was happy with that grade. I didn't want to hear him saying, "Why can't you pull that grade up to an A?" Daddy had to laugh about that statement. He said, "If you are satisfied, then I am too." I was so glad when that semester was *over.*

Graduation day arrived! I would be going to Garnet High School in the fall.

Garnet High School

Finally, the day arrived I would be entering Garnet High School in the fall of 1952. It was a wonderful day graduating from junior high but nothing like graduating from Garnet High. Words cannot express how I felt when I walked up the stairs and entered the building. I was elated to be following in Mary Goldie's footsteps. Most of my friends who had older brothers or sisters who attended or graduated from Garnet felt the same way.

As I entered Garnet, I couldn't believe how immaculately clean the floors were. They looked like shiny mirror. The environment was pleasant. The culture was positive. We all knew why we were there: to get an education. Students respected the teachers and their school. We walked the halls proudly, orderly and quietly. We had excellent teachers. They were caring and always had a positive attitude. Of course, some of them knew Daddy. One of his former classmates taught brick mason classes. As I said before, we all knew what our ultimate goal was: get that diploma. Then go on to college. My curriculum was college preparatory.

Everyday in our homerooms we began the day with scripture and prayer. Chief Moore was my homeroom and biology teacher. We took turns selecting a scripture or offering the prayer. Sometimes Chief Moore offered the prayer. We had to go over our homework, especially our biology homework, before we were dismissed for our classes.

As I said before, our teachers were wonderful. I loved Mr. Barnes' English Literature classes. His favorite poet was William Shakespeare. He loved acting out the roles of Romeo and Juliet. He also liked Milton, Emily Dickinson and Edgar Allen Poe.

Mr. Davis taught French with a passion. His sister, Miss Mays, taught art. Mr. Jarrett taught history and physical education. Patricia *loved* his history classes. Even today she talks about his classes. All the male teachers wore suits and ties. However, Mr. Barnes and Mr. Jarrett stood out above the crowd. They were *"sharp"* impeccable dressers.

Mrs. Ruth S. Norman taught English. She was also the director of the Senior Boys and Girls Speech Choirs. We appeared throughout the city at various functions (black and white), school assemblies, radio stations and on television. I still remember some of the scriptures we memorized: Psalm 1—Blessed is the man that walketh not in the counsel of the ungodly. Psalm 24-The earth is the Lord's. Psalm 91—He that dwelleth in the secret place of the most high. Psalm 100—Make a joyful noise unto the Lord, all ye lands. Psalm 121—I will lift up mine eyes unto the hills, from whence cometh my help . . .

Some of the scriptures the girls presented and some the boys presented. Then Mrs. Norman selected scriptures we presented as combined choirs.

The Holy Bible, Old and New Testaments in the King James Version (1976). Pasadena, California: Thru the Bible Radio

Mrs. Norman was one of my most admired teachers. Though she was small in stature. She walked with an air of authority. "When you are walking always look as if you are going somewhere" was her motto.

Mrs. India Harris was the director of the Glee Club and the Girls Ensemble. She had a sweet personality. She always spoke in a quiet soft voice. I was a member of the Girls Ensemble as well as the Future Teachers of America and the Student Council. We sang throughout the city of Charleston and the surrounding areas.

Mrs. Josephine Rayford and Mr. Maceo Brown taught business education. Mrs. Rayford was Mary Goldie's teacher and coach when she competed with other students from Bluefield, Mt. Hope, and Elkhorn, West Virginia. Garnet always won first or second in most categories at the Annual State High School Commercial Contest. The students competed in the areas of shorthand, typing, bookkeeping, and business arithmetic.

Mrs. Rayford and Mr. Nelson were named West Virginia's "Commercial Teachers of the Year-1955." Needless to say, I did not excel in this area. However, I did earn a B for this course. These were a few of the teachers who really impacted my life.

As I mentioned earlier, I was involved in several activities when Homer Davis, the president of the Student Council, asked if he could submit my name on the slate of nominees for the election of Miss Garnet. I asked him if he was he kidding! He was not, so reluctantly I said, "okay". The candidates had to give a speech before the entire school in the auditorium the day before the election. Yvonne Jackson was elected Miss Garnet. Irene Dabney and I were elected her attendants. Homer was beaming when he congratulated me before the winners were announced. I was surprised. We would be representing our school at various functions as well as attending sport events. I was amazed Daddy permitted me to run because we had these obligations

Three years passed so quickly before I knew it, graduation day was here. One day I noticed that certain students were being summoned to the principal's office.

Each time a student returned to class they would tap the shoulder of another student to go to Mr. Dennis' office. When Wilson Willard told me I was next I was surprised. Not one of the students mentioned why he or she was summoned. When I walked into the secretary's office I was filled with much apprehension. Miss Carrie M. Richards, the secretary, asked me why I looked the way I did when I entered her office? Smiling, she assured me that I did not have anything to worry about. When I entered Mr. Harris's office he smiled and said congratulations! "Congratulations for what?" You are graduating with honors. I was the fourth honoree! He said with caution, this ranking could change before graduation. You could have knocked me over with a feather. I knew the ranking would remain the same because the grades were already in. I couldn't wait to get home to tell my parents. They were so proud of my accomplishment.

There was such a buzz in the Rush household as we prepared to attend the Graduation. I was the first to graduate from high school. I could hardly wait to get my diploma. After singing in the Ensemble, listening to the Glee Club and the guest speaker, *finally* diplomas were presented. When I heard my name called I floated across the stage. My head was held high and my chest was sticking out with pride as my family applauded and screamed my name. That was one of my proudest days, now on to college.

Graduation Day - Westfield State College

Chapter 10

Desegregation and Integration

When the desegregation law passed in 1955 I had just graduated from Garnet High. It was a bittersweet victory. Daddy felt that desegregation would destroy a lot of our culture and accomplishments. My future brother-in-law, Thomas (Homer's brother) was a member of the last graduating class, as well as Carl, from Garnet in 1956. It was such a sad day for everyone, parents and students alike. Though our level of educational standards was higher than the white school Daddy believed all the black schools should be brought up to the same standards as the white schools. "Give all the schools the same text books, supplies and equipment." he said. Daddy did not think it was right to close down *all* the black schools, especially Garnet High School, which was one of *the best* schools in Charleston, West Virginia. Our Boyd Junior High School was completely torn down. For years all that was left was a big empty space until a trucking company started parking their rigs there. Daddy stated that the schools should be integrated by having school choice. Students should be able to attend any school of their choice. "What if the Whites don't want to go to a black school?" "What if Blacks don't want to go to a white school?" we asked? His response was, "They would *have that choice and* you would have a choice also."

Anyway you cannot make people do anything they do not want to do. It's against their nature. *Just make all the schools equal."*

Nothing was saved from dear old Garnet High. Everything was destroyed or placed on the curb for rubbish: trophies, books, graduating class pictures. Homer, my husband, was passing by Garnet when this happened. He was able to salvage our graduating class picture and Mary Goldie's husband's class picture.

I recall reading an article in the Charleston, West Virginia's Beacon Digest. The headline was WVU Holds Black High School 'Family Reunion.' Former principals, students, coaches and friends attended. They talked about sports in segregated and integrated schools. The panel shared experiences of coaches and principals who were not given comparative positions, cheerleaders and majorettes overlooked in competition and students having to adjust to a lower value system. Students were grouped lower than their ability assessment or having to overcome prejudice in selection of students to first string positions. Coaches were not utilized in their professions many of them went into the classrooms.

Gilmer, A.E. (2005, April 20). WVU Holds Black High School 'Family Reunion.' *West Virginia Beacon Digest,* p 1

The concerns held by parents for their children entering all white schools the following year were valid one. Students were denied first team positions previously held in sports, cheerleading and band. Elementary children were not encouraged to play in games on the schoolyards.

Until this day, Tishy is bitter because she did not graduate from Garnet High. In fact all of her friends feel the same way today. They missed all the comradeship their brothers and sisters had. As I stated before, all the little brothers and sisters wanted to attend Garnet just as their siblings before them.

Even today, Tishy often speaks about the feeling of displacement as she entered Charleston High School in the eleventh grade. The school's culture was totally different from Garnet's. The building was not kept clean. There was chaos in the hallways. Everything was opposite of how Garnet operated. At Garnet we had a routine that was followed everyday. Walking in the hallways, keeping your voices down; enter the classroom in an orderly manner. Every morning we met with our homeroom teacher for morning devotion: prayer and scripture before attending our classes. Our teachers really cared about each and every one of the students.

When Tishy entered Charleston High she was a year educationally ahead of the white students. That's because we had great teachers who instilled in all of us the importance of getting an education. Our teachers knew that we had to be prepared to compete, at the highest level, in our society.

Tishy couldn't remember the name of her former Garnet classmate, who had a higher GPA than the white student for the Valedictorian. This classmate from Garnet High received *special recognition* for her GPA. Tishy was awarded a $750 scholarship from Frankenburger's Department Store. When she applied for admission to West Virginia State College (today it's West Virginia State University) she was given a four years scholarship after the bursar verified her grades. Daddy was right after all about school choice. Integration was *great* for the whites because they flocked to West Virginia State College the following year after the desegregation law passed. We were astonished! And it is still like this even today as I write this book. West Virginia State College University WSCU, the name was change a couple years ago, is one of the best colleges in the state of West Virginia.

Chapter 11

Daddy's Only Love

Daddy worshiped the ground Mama walked upon. He couldn't keep his hands off her. He often talked about when they first met. Her figure was like an hourglass. She was beautiful and still is today. "All of you girls are pretty. But none of you are as beautiful as your mother," he'd say when he finished describing Mama. I was fifteen or sixteen when I thought, Wow, Daddy acted as if he and Mama were teenagers. When I read his letters to her they are full of his love for her. He wrote to her every week when he was working away from home. Now they weren't perfect. They did have a few differences. Mama spoke up when she needed to speak. I never heard them argue or raise their voices at each other. Mama had a sweet, soft nature. She was quiet until she did not think Daddy was right. Then she would speak up in her quiet firm manner. That's the reason why her death was so difficult for him. I will never forget the day she passed, I had a dream, vision, or premonition the night before Mama's death. I shrugged it off the next morning but as I recalled, Mama was never ill. Daddy was working in Ohio. I dreamed that I went to school as I was now in college. In my dream it was one o'clock and I walked out of class to catch the bus for home. I had an urgent need to get there. Mama was very ill! I rushed her to the hospital. Oh, this is just a dream but I couldn't shake the foreboding feeling.

I watched Mama prepare our breakfast with a funny feeling hanging over me. I kept looking at her. She seemed okay. I left the house to catch the bus to college.

Classes were fine until one o'clock. I believe I was in psychology class. I became very agitated. I tried to remain in my seat but I just couldn't. I jumped up and started to leave the room. The professor asked me where I was going. I replied, "Home." I ran to the bus stop. The bus was coming. I was perspiring. I could hardly breathe as if I had been running for a mile. I thought the bus couldn't get me home fast enough. And this was not a dream. It was real!

Mrs. Kitchen, our next-door neighbor was with Mama. Mama was so ill vomiting and complaining about her stomach. Mrs. Kitchen advised me to get my mother to the hospital immediately. I kept asking Mama what was wrong? She couldn't answer because she was in so much pain. I got Mama to the hospital by ambulance. After a while the doctors told me that they would do an exploratory surgery the next day at one o'clock. I went home. Mrs. Edith, Mrs. Kitchen's sister was there also. She told me to call Daddy right away. I was numb and moving in a fog. My mind was like jelly. I couldn't think clearly. I called Daddy after I knew he'd finished working. I was sobbing and telling him that he had to come home now! The doctors scheduled the operation for one o'clock the next day. I contacted my Grandmother Gogo, Mama's mother and Aunt Marie; they all arrived later that evening.

In the meantime Patricia arrived home from school. Already I was beginning to have a feeling of loneliness. That foreboding feeling was strong. I didn't tell anyone about the dream. The house seemed to already have the feel of emptiness.

Daddy drove all night from Columbus, Ohio. He arrived around twelve thirty and went directly to the hospital. Gogo, our grandmother was already at the hospital. The older siblings waited at home with Aunt Marie, Mrs. Kitchen and Mrs. Edith. Suzette and Charles were sent to school. When Daddy entered the house we knew that Mama was gone. I heard Mrs. Kitchen and Mrs. Edith say in unison, "Oh no!" Daddy told us that he arrived just as Mama was being taken into the operating room. He was able to speak with her. He told her how much he loved her and he would be waiting for her after the surgery was over. Mama expired on the operating table. The minute the doctor made the incision into her stomach she expired. She had pancreatic cancer. It had spread throughout her body. Oh how Daddy cried and cried. I fell out in the floor screaming and kicking. Mrs. Edith grabbed me and held me real tight. Patricia or Ramona went to pick up Charles and Suzette from School. I will never forget the look in their eyes when they learned of Mama's death. This was the worst day of all of our lives, especially for Suzette and Charles. They were babies. Emptiness had already settled in. What would we do without Mama? What would Daddy do without Mama?

The night after Mama passed I had another dream or vision. I seem to be in a trance when I saw Mama enter the house from the side door. I looked at her in astonishment. There was a bright light around her. Her eyes cautioned me not to say a word. She was wearing her red slip. She walked slowly through our room, through the kitchen and through the added room on the back of the house. Then she exited through the back door. I was soaking wet as I pulled the covers over my eyes. The next day when I told my grandmother of my vision she became frightened. She said that she loved Thelma but she did not want to see her spirit. I was surprised that she was afraid of her *own* daughter's spirit.

We were all functioning in a fog preparing for Mama's funeral. In those days the deceased were viewed in their homes. Mama's coffin was placed in our living-room for the wake. After everyone left Daddy sat by her coffin all night. He took pictures of her lying in her coffin. I could never bring myself to look at those photos. He kept them in his scrapbook until the day he passed.

When the minister said Mr. Rush is now reunited with his wife Thelma. I couldn't believe we said "Yea" in unison. We were just so happy that Daddy was finally with his only love again. After the service at the church I couldn't believe all the cars in the processional. There were twenty-five or more. Mama certainly had lots of friends I thought to myself. Some members from Daddy's union also attended. Mama's best friend, Mrs. Garner told us several months later Mama told her that she would never live to move into the house they were building in Dunbar. Did she have a premonition?

After the funeral, our Grandmother Gogo and Aunt Marie moved in because Daddy was still working in Ohio. He gathered us around and told us that no other woman was coming into this house. Zehline will handle the finances and help run the house with your Grandmother. Each week he gave me his paycheck. I took care of all the bills and the banking. We went shopping together on Saturday for groceries just as he and Mama had done. Daddy informed the others when Zehline leaves the next one in line would take over. That's the way it's going to be. Patricia stepped up to the plate when I left.

Chapter 12

The Surprise Birthday Party

Daddy's seventy-fifth birthday was approaching. We, Monie, Charles and I decided to have a surprise party for him. Oh, we knew this would be a challenge for us. I was designated to go to Charleston to visit with Daddy and make all the arrangements along with Charles.

I called Daddy to let him know that I was planning to come for a visit. "Come on that's why I built this house with an extra bedroom so all my children would have a place to stay." I flew in from Massachusetts. Daddy was instrumental in the redevelopment of our old neighborhood. He was written up in the Charleston Gazette for getting the government funds to rebuild the neighborhood. Although he knew I was coming he seemed surprised to see me. We had a great time together visiting during my two week visit.

Charles came a few days later from Cincinnati. He told Daddy he came to see Zehline and of course you, Daddy. Charles and I made all the arrangements. We rented the Ritz Club. It is no longer in existence. We planned the menu. Janice, Charles's spouse would bake the cake, that was her profession. Everything was all set. Then we visited Daddy's former classmates and friends who still lived in St. Albans and Mandeville.

We invited most of his friends who attended the one room schoolhouse with him. We located the friends who attended high school also. One classmate, Mrs. Smith showed us pictures of the old schoolhouse. Roland Hayes was the name of the school. Mrs. Smith was very helpful. She gave us the names of the other classmates and how to reach them. Her sons and I attended Garnet together.

The meeting with Mrs. Smith was educational. It was interesting listening to Daddy's friends and former classmates talk about their days at Roland Hayes School. They were happy and excited to receive an invitation. They commented that it would be something to see Charles again after all these years.

While I was home Daddy took the opportunity of my visit to get his affairs in order. We went to see a lawyer to have his will drawn up. He gave instructions about what to do about the house. It was to be sold and the money distributed equally. No one is to get more than the other. I was to contact his union to collect the money from his insurance. This money would be used for his burial. His statues were to be divided among his children. I was to receive his piano. He also purchased Certificate of Deposits for each sibling. After Daddy completed putting his affairs in order I returned to Massachusetts.

Finally the day arrived, Daddy's seventy-fifth birthday! Everyone arrived a day or two ahead of the party. Homer and I stayed with Mr. and Mrs. Preston. They lived five houses from Daddy's house. Ramona and John drove from Georgia. Patricia and Percy flew in from Las Vegas. Mary Goldie flew in from San Francisco. Suzette and Greg drove from Baltimore. Charles and Janice drove from Cincinnati the day of the party. They went directly to Daddy's house. Daddy was surprised to see them. They told him they came to help him celebrate his seventy-fifth birthday. Daddy wasn't for this. He thanked them saying no thanks. At this time he had a female friend who was in on the surprise birthday party. She helped coax him to go out to dinner with them. Finally Daddy relented. When he walked into the Ritz

Club he was flabbergasted! Later he said to me under his breath "That's why you came last month." I must say he thoroughly enjoyed himself visiting each table chattering with his guests, my siblings and his grandchildren. When he thanked everyone for coming he told them how proud and blessed he was to have such a wonderful family and friends. He spoke about his birthday party frequently. He admitted that he was very happy we had the party for him. He was elated because he was able to reminisce with his former classmates.

Chapter 13

Lessons to Live By

Relatives

Daddy was forever quoting to us "Just because they are some kin, it doesn't mean you have to be lovey-dovey with them." That was Daddy's motto. You don't really know them or how they live. You just don't let everybody come into your home. He reiterated this message to my sister Ramona. Every time a relative, from her husband's side of the family, came to Georgia, they would stop at their house to spend a night or two. Sometimes they would bring a friend or two. Many of John's relatives were not close to him. After Daddy talked with Monie and John about allowing relatives to take advantage of them, the word got around about dropping in on the Hailey family. These relatives soon got the message that John and Ramona's home was not an oasis. Monie told me about one of John's cousins calling when he arrived in town, telling her that he wanted to spend a couple of nights. He had his family and a friend with him. Monie informed him that she would gladly help him get a hotel room nearby. She said that cousin blessed her out. No more uninvited guests. The word passed quickly.

I, too, learned a lesson about relatives. One lesson was a pleasant one and the other proved that Daddy was always right.

When I was around ten years old I became interested in our family tree. I often questioned Daddy about his relatives down south.

We all knew that his father had to leave Alabama because his father killed a white man in self-defense. I wrote about this earlier in the book. Daddy often talked about Uncle Charlie back home. As a result, I started corresponding with Uncle Charlie. I was surprised when he answered back. We corresponded back and forth for a year or more. One day I received a letter telling me that Uncle Charlie and his wife were coming to Charleston for a visit. I couldn't wait to show the letter to Daddy when he came home from work. I never thought that they would be staying with us in our little overcrowded house. They did. I also didn't know what to expect with regard to how Uncle Charlie would look. He was short in stature and his hair was gray, completely gray. He looked to me like Uncle Remus in the movies. We didn't talk much as he and Daddy had lots of catching up to do.

One morning, I came around the side of the house. Uncle Charlie and his wife were sitting in the swing on the front porch. I purposely came that way because I did not want to speak. I *hated* to say good morning for some reason. I maintained that awful attitude into my adult life. Don't ask me why? Anyway, Uncle Charlie asked me, "Did I sleep with you last night?" I was taken aback by that question. In fact, I was shocked that a grown man would say something like that to a child. I replied indignantly, "No and why would you ask me something like that?' His response was," Listen young lady, it's proper to speak to a person when you get up in the morning." Offhandedly I replied, "Oh, Good morning. "That's better," was his response. Toward the end of their two weeks visit I began to warm up to him. That's when he told Daddy he would give each of us an acre of land if we came for a visit. Uncle George allowed George Henry to travel by Greyhound bus for a visit. Of course, Daddy did not allow any of his girls to visit. Before we could blink an eye George Henry was back in Charleston. Uncle Charlie sent him back because he had sassed a white man at the gas station. Uncle Charlie said things were different down south. He had to live there. He felt that George Henry had a fresh mouth. That was the end of receiving any land in Alabama.

Daddy had another relative, a cousin in Detroit, Michigan. Although he knew about her he did not know her very well. Once again I found her address and began corresponding with her. I corresponded with this adult cousin for over a year. I was in the sixth grade when she invited me to come to visit her during the summer.

Daddy kept telling me that I did not know anything about this cousin every time I begged him to let me go to Detroit. "Just because she is some kin does not mean she lives the same way you do. You just don't jump up and go somewhere without knowing something about them". I kept begging and begging.

One day, Daddy's no became a yes. We all crowded into the car with our suitcases packed in the trunk. Then off we went to Detroit. We were excited! I was on cloud nine! Mary Goldie, Patricia and I chattered part of the way or slept part of the way. When we finally arrived at the cousin's house, my face fell. She did not live in a nice neighborhood, not like mine. That's when Tishy said under her breathe," You're staying *here* all summer?' I was very quiet. I looked up at the house and thought, "This was the biggest house I had ever seen." The house was two stories and needed lots of care. The door was wide open without a screen. Later I learned that this was a boarding house. There were three men sitting on the front porch drinking beer early in the morning. Daddy asked about his cousin. I heard one of the men say, "Yeah, yeah, yeah, she's in there," pointing towards the front door. Daddy went inside. A few minutes later he returned with his cousin. She stood in the doorway smiling and beckoned for us to come in. He called, "Come on, Zehline." I wasn't happy about this situation which I had begged for. I hung back as we walked up five or six steps. I discovered that this was a boarding house as Daddy and I walked down a long dark hallway with lots of doors on each side. Finally, we entered our cousin's apartment. I stood behind Daddy as my cousin tried to talk to me. She couldn't even pronounce my name. All I could think about was *"I'm not staying here!"*

Mama and Daddy visited for an hour or so. Daddy stood up. It's time to go, I thought to myself and I am *ready!* I eased over beside Daddy and said to him in a low voice, "I'm not staying here." Daddy (ignoring me) said he would get my suitcase. I ran back to the car. Daddy kept urging me to come on as he pretended to get my suitcase. I started to cry. Tishy hissed to me, "You're staying here," as she jumped into the car claiming my seat by the window. Finally after a few minutes of Daddy's bantering, Mama had enough. She told Daddy to stop teasing me and told me to get into the car. Daddy began fussing, telling me he ought to make me stay. "Now you see exactly what I have been telling you about wanting to stay with a relative just because they are some kin." "What would you have done if I had sent you here on the bus or train alone?" "Now let this be a lesson to you: all of you to remember." I did not care how Daddy spoke to me or how long he dwelled on the subject. I was elated because I *didn't* get my wish. My parents had planned in advance to visit Mama's cousins. This was an opportunity for Daddy to teach me as well as my sisters a real life lesson.

Crabs in a Barrel

Throughout Daddy's life, he told us how he observed and listened to people. He wasn't happy how we as a race did not pull together. He used the example of watching crabs in a barrel. "Whenever one crab gets almost to the top of the barrel, all the others crabs would reach up and pull it back into the barrel. Not one of them was able to get out of the barrel. We have got to learn to help each other," he said. "We could have our own hospitals and businesses if we worked together. Instead of us being proud of the person's accomplishments, we begin to talk about the person. They think they are so smart because of this or that. They could do the same thing if they applied themselves. Every failure you have is not the other man's fault. If you get a bag of lemons in life, turn it around and make some lemonade. Then sell it".

Today some black athletes have started businesses and organizations to help others. We still have a long way to go.

Water Maiden.

Borrowing

Daddy did not believe in borrowing for any reason. His motto was "Do without until you are able to get what you want." He did not allow us to borrow each other's clothes, and that was all right with me. However; Tishy wore her clothes and everyone else's. She was such a tomboy. She would ruin her clothes and then switch them for one of our clothes. We each had a designated drawer for our clothes. Tishy would put her ruined clothes in one of our drawers. Then she would replace it with something of ours but Mama always knew that the ruined clothes were Tishy's.

Buying on Time
Layaway

Layaway was Daddy's way of purchasing things he wanted. He would tell us, "When I get it out, it's all mine, and I don't owe anyone anything." I recall when Daddy purchased two rings on layaway. One had a ruby setting; this was his birthstone. The other ring had a diamond setting. He proudly displayed each one on his finger when he brought them home after the final payment. "They are all mine, I don't owe anyone anything," he proclaimed. Charles inherited the rings after Daddy's death. Daddy also purchased Mama a white gold (platinum) watch when I was in the second grade on layaway. I have the watch today. We all followed Daddy's example. I purchased all my school clothes and shoes when I entered high school, using layaway. After I married I purchased many things also on layaway.

Save for a Rainy Day

Daddy believed in saving, no matter how small the amount. Save 10 percent of everything you earn or money you get for birthday gifts. Every little bit adds up. Every week, he would put money in a locked drawer in our bedroom. He kept silver coins in a large piggy bank on the mantle in his bedroom. One summer evening, Daddy said to Mama, "Thelma, let's see how much we've saved." When Mama came back into the living room with the piggy bank, a few coins were clinking on the sides of the bank as she shook it. There couldn't have been anymore than three or four quarters in it. She kept shaking it as we heard *ting-a-ling ting-a-ling*. Daddy was shocked! "Thelma, what happened to all the money?"

"I spent it on things that we needed," she replied. We all sat looking at Mama in awe with our mouths open and our eyes wide open as an owl. Needless to say, the same scenario happened with the locked drawer. Mama did use the money wisely. Daddy was dumbfounded. He didn't get angry. He looked as if he was hurt. I was surprised. He just hung his head.

As we grew older and had family gatherings, Daddy always retold the story about the "missing" money. He would always laugh and laugh about it. However, Daddy started saving in the bank. It was my job to take the deposit to the bank each week. To this day, I save 10 percent or more from monies I receive. Of course, 10 percent goes to my church.

Another piece of advice concerning our finances Daddy told us to pay our rent, pay our tithes and pay ourselves first. Don't give all your money on monthly account. If you ever fall behind go to the owner and work out a plan to repay the account with reduced payments.

Learn by Watching

Daddy told us that he learned more by listening and watching others. He was very good doing them both. He learned how to draw and sculpt himself. Some of his artwork was displayed in the State Capitol in Charleston, West Virginia, and in New York at the Empire State Building. Oh, we were so excited when Daddy and Mama went to New York just to see if his work was on display. Our grandmother and Aunt Marie came to stay with us while they were gone for the weekend. They rode the train to New York. We were beaming proudly as we excitedly waited for our parents' arrival on Sunday. Daddy's face was radiant when he shared how he felt when he saw his statues on display in the Empire State Building. He announced, "They *really were* there!" They brought us little replicas of the Statue of Liberty. We showed them to all our friends in the neighborhood.

Never Sell your Vote

This was really one of Daddy's pet peeves. Every year at election time the white men (Mr. Charlie) would come into the neighborhood looking for people to vote. They were *nice and friendly* urging people to vote and giving them rides to the polls. They also went to Court Street to pick up the winos to vote. This was the "good ole boy tactic". The "voters" were shown which box to mark and when they voted they received a fifth of liquor. Daddy tried to get them not to throw away their vote. "Study the issues," he'd say. "Then decide which candidate is best for you and the majority of the people." Their response was "Man they giving a fifth of whiskey. I ain't passing *that* up!" Most of them were not registered voters. Until this day we are registered voters. We volunteer for the candidates we feel will help the people and the country. Daddy always told us "Do not vote for a party; vote for the candidate and what they stand for. Never sell your vote for any candidate or party. Learn the issues on both sides. How are they going to help you and the majority of the people? Then you vote and hope that candidate will follow through on the things he ran for".

Lessons to Live By

The Ladder of Life

As we advanced in our education Daddy believed that we could always better ourselves. "Associate with people who are a little smarter than you. Learn from them. You can't learn from someone who is at the same level you are. Just don't think you are ever better than someone else. Learn all you can about everything. Just remember as you advance up the ladder of success (life) the same people you passed going up may be the same people you'll pass going down: just be yourselves".

We were advised to always sit near the front of the classroom, not in the back. "You'll have less distraction when others are not focus. You will learn more".

Set Goals

Daddy believed in setting goals. He'd say, "Take tiny steps," demonstrating about an inch with his finger and thumb. "Reach that goal then set another then another until you get to that ultimate goal". You'll have set backs along the way. This will help you to become stronger and more determined to reach that ultimate goal. *Never* give up. "You will always learn from each set back. "They are your challenges".

Strength in Numbers

We were in the kitchen one evening when Daddy came home. We were arguing with our cousins George Henry and Bobby. The argument was getting heated. That's when Daddy ordered everyone to sit down. "Families stick together no matter what. We do not need to have strife among ourselves. When you are divided your strength is weakened. All of you should be pulling together and not pulling against each other." He took a package of spaghetti from the kitchen cabinet. He pulled one piece of spaghetti from the box and easily broke it in half. Then he demonstrated how difficult it was to break a bunch of spaghetti.

"Now you can see when you stay together you have strength in number. If one of you decides to go off by yourself you won't have the strength you would have with your family. Always stick together".

Marriage

When you marry you and your husband should always work as a team. Make decisions together. You don't let anyone come between you. Most of all don't let any man mistreat you or take advantage of you. This is why I encouraged each of you to get your education because I don't want you to be beholden to any man. If or when you come to a fork in the road and can't agree which path to take together, take time to find a solution. And if a solution cannot be found, then take the road that is best for *you*. Each of you will be able to take care of yourselves. This is truly a fact.

We were also advised to never have women visiting our homes all the time, especially if you are not home. Things can happen when women hang around your husband. Don't allow an opportunity for someone to move in on your territory. Marriage is a lifetime commitment. It's up to you and your husband to make your marriage work.

Fashions

Daddy always dressed. He kept his clothes neatly pressed and his shoes polished. He also had a pair of brown crepe sole suede shoes he brushed off before putting them in the box before placing them in the closet. He explained the importance of always keeping our clothes clean so they are ready when you need them.

Just because a fashion or the style is in, it does not mean that it is for you. You dress according to how the clothes you wear look good on you. Don't look ridiculous just to be in style. Hemlines go up and down all the time; you find the length that looks best on you. If it does not look good on you, don't wear it and look ridiculous.

"The majority of these styles are not for everybody. Keep the length that looks best on you no matter how many times the hemline is raised or lowered. Simplicity is the answer. If you buy simple, quality clothing, you will never go out of style". Today I still have skirts that are back in style, especially the tweed jacket and gray skirt with four kick pleats in the back (Mama-made). My daughter Renè wore some of my clothes when she was in high school. Simplicity and quality are the answers to being fashionable. You can dress an outfit up with accessories: a scarf, a belt, or a piece of jewelry to make that dress look different each time you wear it. Wow, Daddy didn't miss a thing. He also told us, "I don't care if you have only one dress and one set of undergarments, keep them clean. Wash them every night and be ready the next day." Thank you, Daddy for another valuable piece of advice. You were so right as usual.

Daddy had a long camel hair coat which he wore it every winter. Each time he wore this coat and those brown suede shoes he always received so many compliments. People wanted to know where he had gotten them. This was an example that some styles do not ever become dated. He had this coat and those shoes from when I was in the second or third grade and through my college years.

Mama felt the same way about her clothes. Now you know there wasn't any reason for us not to follow suit. We all followed in their footsteps. I particularly love Mama more for making my clothes because I did not want anyone to have the same outfits I wore. Daddy was great in designing outfits as we became older. People could not believe the fabulous clothes Mama made for us. She stayed up many nights sewing for the five of us. As I have said before, we all love clothes and shoes until this day.

Grocery Shopping

Every Saturday Mama and Daddy went grocery shopping at the A&P. One day I asked Daddy why they always waited until just about closing time to go. "That's when you get all the marked down items, especially the meat. I get the same brands at a reduced price, bread, milk, etc. I save a lot of money this way". (Not today, it will be close to the expiration date before an item is marked down.)

My parents were very frugal shoppers. Mama and Daddy came home with bags and bags of groceries. Seriously, the back seat of the car was packed as well as the trunk.

Sometimes Carl would help to take the groceries inside the house. We had our favorite food on Saturdays: hamburgers with all the trimmings. My girl friend, Carol Seals lived next door. Miss Edith was her grandmother. She told me after we were adults that she always waited for my parents to come home after shopping. She always ran as fast as she could to help us carry the groceries into the house. "I wanted to get one of those hamburger sandwiches your mother made. I never heard of salad dressing on a hamburger before," as she laughed. All of us loved Spanish bar cake. Even today the recipe flavor of the Spanish bar cake cannot be duplicated even by the A&P bakery. They were so delicious! I loved the icing also.

Friends and Acquaintances

We were cautioned about having too many friends or so-called friends. You only need one or two close friends you can trust and rely upon. The rest of your "friends" are your acquaintances. You don't tell anyone or everyone your business unless you want it out in the streets. However, treat everyone right, be cordial. You'll have fewer heartaches and confusion.

Live Within Your Means

"Do without" was another of Daddy's mottos. He would drill that into our heads constantly. Just because Susie and John are buying all kinds of things; you don't go out and get in debt just to keep up with "The Jones." Live within in your means. Buy what you can afford. Buy what you need. If Susie and John are making Fifty thousand dollars I bet they are spending seventy or eighty thousand. Things are not always what they seem. Live within your means and you will have less stress in your life.

Chapter 14

General Thoughts and Predictions

The only other time I saw Daddy so profoundly grief stricken was on the death of Dr. Martin Luther King, Jr. His assassination affected him just as it did when Mama passed. He couldn't believe it just like everyone else. He admired Dr. King (that's how he always addressed him when he spoke of him.) Daddy admired his courage and tenacity in spite of all the opposition he faced. He was a brave man. Dr. King was fighting for equal rights for all men. He wanted all men to be treated equal. He would tell us.

I recall Daddy saying "I don't know if I could do it: people spitting on you, dogs biting on you and being called out of your name. I don't know if I could do it". When he saw the destruction the people were causing on television; rioting, looting and setting buildings on fire. He hung his head and cried. He kept repeating, "Why in the world would the people destroy their homes, their neighborhoods, shops and other people's businesses? Don't they know that it will be *years*, if ever, before their neighborhoods will be rebuilt?" Rioting was happening on the east and the west coasts. It was disgusting when we watched men and young boys breaking into stores taking food, clothing or anything they could get their hands on. They were grinning and laughing all the while taking merchandise that did not belong to them. Daddy kept saying "Dr. King would not approve of this kind of behavior. This is against everything he has tried to accomplish".

Another thing that bothered Daddy: neighborhoods that were not kept clean. "Why do people live in squalor and filth? Why do people let their neighborhoods get this way? When you see paper or a bottle on the ground pick it up. It doesn't matter who put it there. It's your neighborhood also. There isn't any reason anyone should allow where they live to become filthy. Then wait for someone to come in and clean up after them".

Earlier I mentioned how we had to clean the whole house, yard, the sidewalk and the curb if he found a piece of paper on the floor or in the yard. Every neighbor in the neighborhood swept the sidewalk in front of their homes and picked up paper thrown down by someone walking through the neighborhood. Another of Daddy's motto was "The first impression is a lasting impression." "The inside of the house could be as neat as a pin and the outside is not. What do you think the person will remember? They will always remember the appearance of the untidy yard or how the entrance looked when they arrived." Another saying of his was "Its easier to do things right the first time rather than repeating the same task over and over again." Always learn to do things right the first time."

Now Daddy's thoughts will be controversial to some of you. However, these are his thoughts and opinions.

- He believed our government revealed too much information. "You don't hear other nations blabbing everything they are planning or doing. Our media puts this country in jeopardy everyday competing to be the first to reveal what the government is doing. Some things we do not need to know until it has happened or the plan is finished".

- The United States cannot police the whole world. We need to take care of our own affairs before we enter another man's country to tell them how to live and treat their fellow man. Charity begins at home.

- Yes, there will be a black man in the White House. I may not live to see it but he's coming.

- The United States will not be destroyed by another country. We will do this all by ourselves. Our country is going to fall from within. Greed will bring this country to its knees.

- I wouldn't be surprised if eventually people will be living in caves again. Man is destroying the environment everyday.

- "Rome was a mighty nation at one time. Look at it now. They aren't a threat to anyone today. The same thing can happen to this country. It will take God's help to turn things around."

- There will be so many health problems because of the ingredients, chemicals and preservatives in packaged foods. He told us this when the first packaged food by Betty Crocker was shown on television (on black and white TV.) Now, you know how long ago that was. Chickens were injected in the necks with something to fatten them up. He saw this when he worked at a poultry business. He also worked in a cattle slaughtering house. These predictions are coming true. I heard on ABC news while writing this book (June 2010) sugar is being injected into the breast of chickens. Increasing salt intake in certain foods increases more cravings for that particular food. It's really the salt. We have learned that this is to get the consumers to crave the products.

These predictions are coming true.

Chapter 15

Daddy's Final Journey

When Daddy closed his eyes for the last time I felt so guilty for many, many years because I did not get to his bedside before he passed. Charles was with him. He called me to tell me that Daddy really wanted to see me. How soon could I get there? This is why I cannot write much about Daddy's passing. I did not get to his bedside in time. When Charles met me at the airport the first thing he said was, "He's gone."

Daddy passed away from black lung disease and heart failure Patricia (Tishy) wrote and read

"A Tribute to Daddy"—May 12, 1991

Our father, how can I begin to tell you about our father? He was wise, caring, understanding, considerate, generous, and strict—very strict, *and* sometimes lenient. Although heartbroken when our mother passed, he did not desert his flock of six children. When people offered to help by breaking up the family, he said "No, we're going to stay a family." He instilled in this children pride, dignity, and high self-esteem. He stressed to us to always keep a goal and strive to be the best that you can be, to set your goals high and strive to meet every challenge, and to keep our chins up. Daddy struggled to educate each of us. He was proud and praised us for our accomplishments. He taught us how to embrace life; take the knocks and bumps and how to roll with the punches. One of his sayings was "Life is what you make it. You can make your bed hard or you can make your bed soft, either way, you have to lie down in it. You have the choice." He'd say "There isn't anything that you can't do if you set your mind to it. All you've got to do is to keep trying." As we begin to mature and we all went our separate ways, whenever, we come together we always talk about how smart Daddy was, and how we see what he meant when he would tell us about different situations. It's funny how now our eyes have become his. We see and know what he was telling us about today. Daddy was a go-getter, made negative things become positives. He'd say, "You've got to take the bitter along with the sweet, that's life." Daddy was bright, intelligent, and ahead of his time.

Thank you, Daddy for a job well done. We all appreciate what a fine job you have done. You are the one we love and appreciate. A poem we have selected which sums you up well is entitled "You are the One." (Unfortunately this poem has been misplaced.)

Daddy will always live in our hearts. Each time we accomplish a goal in our lives, we think about our father and thank him for every sacrifice and everything he taught us. The main one being; how to be successful in everything we do. Thank you, Daddy, for everything you said and demonstrated to us how to cope with life and be a success.

We will always love you.

Daddy's own hands

When he passed away, fifteen years ago, several men from his union spoke to me about his good works and what a great man he was. He was respected and admired for the life he led and the work he had done.

Made in the USA
Lexington, KY
14 November 2010